ínspirations

MOSAICS

20 decorative projects for the home

ínspirations

MOSAICS

20 decorative projects for the home

HELEN BAIRD

PHOTOGRAPHY BY DEBI TRELOAR

LORENZ BOOKS

First published in 1998 by Lorenz Books

© Anness Publishing Limited 1998

Lorenz Books is an imprint of
Anness Publishing Limited
Hermes House
88–89 Blackfriars Road
London SE1 8HA

This edition published in the USA by Lorenz Books, Anness Publishing Inc.,
27 West 20th Street, New York, NY 10011; (800) 354-9657

This edition distributed in Canada by Raincoast Books
8680 Cambie Street, Vancouver, British Columbia V6P 6M9

ISBN 1 85967 751 7

A CIP catalogue record for this book is available from the British Library

Publisher: Joanna Lorenz
Designer: Julie Francis
Jacket Designer: Linda Freeman
Illustrator: Lucinda Ganderton
Photographer: Debi Treloar
Step Photographer: Rodney Forte
Stylist: Labeena Ishaque

Printed in Hong Kong/China

1 3 5 7 9 10 8 6 4 2

MEASUREMENTS

Both imperial and metric measurements have been given in the text. Where conversions produce an awkward number, these
have been rounded for convenience, but will produce an accurate result if one system is used throughout.

CONTENTS

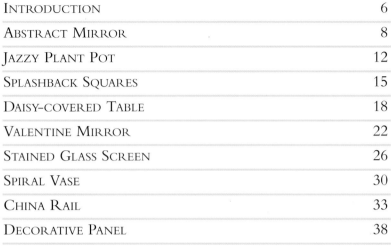

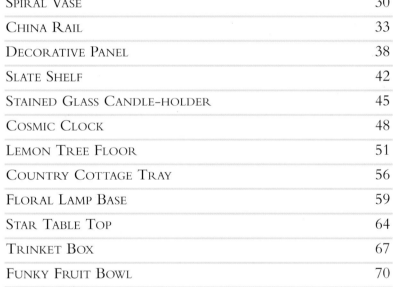

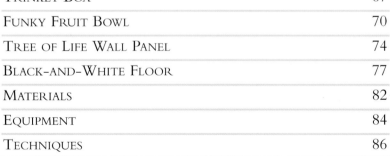

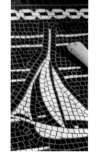

INTRODUCTION

A FEW YEARS AGO, I visited a Roman villa in France, which had stunning mosaic floors. It was hard to believe that they were centuries old. The colours were faded but still beautiful and each piece had been individually cut to create exactly the right shape. However, their delicate appearance was deceptive, in fact the mosaics were made from the hardest of materials, the secret of their long survival.

Whilst the earliest surviving mosaics date back to 3000 BC and are found in present-day Iraq, which was once ancient Mesopotamia, we often associate mosaics with the ancient Romans. Not only did the Romans use mosaics extensively throughout their Empire, but they also perfected the art of mosaic-making, using more durable materials than their predecessors. It was mosaics from the ancient world that inspired the most amazing mosaic that I have ever seen – the indoor swimming pool at San Simeon, Randoph Hearst's house in California. Deep blue tiles with gold pieces dropped in randomly created a dazzling and memorable effect.

We are not suggesting that you try to tackle anything as large in this book but we do have plenty of innovative ideas, ranging from designs for floors to mosaic glass screens and even a clock. My particular favourite is a pale pink table with scattered daisies.

With over twenty projects, each with clear step-by-step instructions, you will be able to choose a project to suit your abilities and the materials available to you – be it mosaic tiles, pieces of slate, broken floor tiles or smashed crockery.

Deborah Barker

ABSTRACT MIRROR

Create your own abstract frame using the semi-indirect method of mosaics. This way, you can arrange the tesserae on paper first, before committing yourself to the final design.

YOU WILL NEED

circular wooden board, 40 cm (16 in) diameter, with a
5 mm (¼ in) lip
brown paper
pair of compasses (compass)
pencil
scissors
circle of mirror glass, 20 cm (8 in) diameter
black marker pen
masking tape
protective goggles
vitreous glass mosaic tesserae
tile nippers
water-soluble glue and brush
craft knife
rubber (latex) gloves
tile grout
mixing bowl
sponge
cement-based tile adhesive
fine-toothed notched spreader
silicone-based adhesive

1 Using a pair of compasses (compass), draw a circle on brown paper 2 mm (¹/₁₂ in) smaller than the wooden board. Cut out. Place the mirror in the centre and draw around it in black pen. Divide the border into eight equal sections. Draw a design clearly in each section.

2 Place the mirror face down in the centre of the paper and attach with a curl of masking tape.

8

3 Wearing protective goggles, cut the tesserae to size with tile nippers. Stick them face down on the paper design, using water-soluble glue. Keep the gaps between the tesserae as even as possible.

4 When the design is complete carefully lower the mosaic on to the board and attach the lip around the outside. Remove the mirror and cut away the brown paper underneath, using a craft knife.

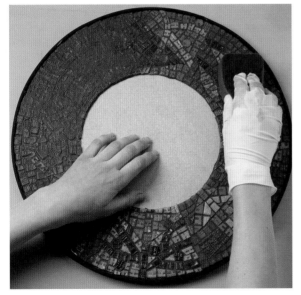

5 Wearing rubber (latex) gloves, rub a small amount of tile grout into the mosaic, then wipe off the excess with a damp sponge. This will bind the tesserae together. Leave until almost dry.

6 Gently remove the mosaic from the board by turning it upside down. Spread the outer area of the board with tile adhesive. Lower the mosaic into the adhesive, mosaic side down, and press firmly.

7 Coat the back of the mirror with silicone-based adhesive and stick the mirror into the centre. Leave to set for 20 minutes.

8 Dampen the paper with a sponge, wait 10 minutes until the glue dissolves, then gently peel it off the mosaic. Clean away any protruding lumps of cement with a damp sponge. Leave to dry, then re-grout, filling in any cracks and sponge clean.

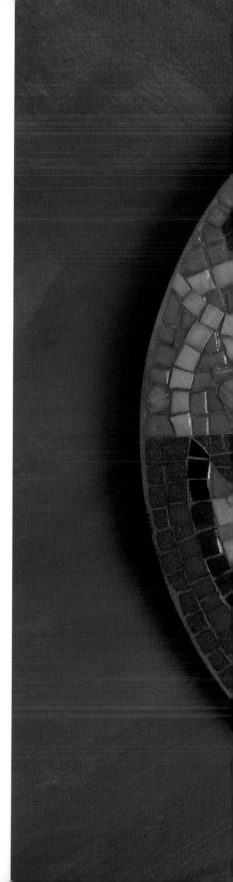

JAZZY PLANT POT

A plain terracotta pot is decorated with squares of brightly coloured tesserae and mirror glass, set in white tile adhesive. Painting the inside with yacht varnish prevents moisture seeping through and loosening the mosaic. Fill with herbs or small cacti.

YOU WILL NEED
small terracotta plant pot
yacht varnish
paintbrush
protective goggles
vitreous glass mosaic tesserae
tile nippers
mirror glass
rubber (latex) gloves
white cement-based tile adhesive
mixing bowl
flexible knife
sponge
dust mask
sandpaper
soft cloth

1 Paint the inside of the plant pot with yacht varnish. Leave to dry.

2 Wearing goggles, cut the tesserae into neat quarters, using tile nippers. Cut small squares of mirror glass the same size, also using tile nippers. Continue cutting the tesserae until you have enough pieces, in a variety of colours, to cover your pot completely.

13

3 Wearing rubber (latex) gloves, mix the tile adhesive as recommended by the manufacturer. Working from the bottom of the pot, spread a thick layer over a small area at a time. Press in the tesserae in rows, including the glass. Leave to dry overnight.

4 Wearing gloves, mix some more tile adhesive and rub all over the surface of the mosaic. Fill any gaps in between the tesserae, then wipe off excess adhesive with a damp sponge before it dries. Again, leave to dry overnight.

5 Wearing a protective dust mask, sand off any lumps of tile adhesive which may have dried on the surface of the mosaic, leaving a smooth surface.

6 Mix some more tile adhesive and smooth over the rim of the pot. Leave until completely dry, then polish with a soft cloth.

SPLASHBACK SQUARES

Mosaic is an ideal surface for decorating bathrooms and kitchens since it is waterproof and easy to wipe clean. This simple design is made of tiles in two colours, alternated to give a checkerboard effect. Choose the colours to match your bathroom fittings.

YOU WILL NEED

12 mm (½ in) thick plywood, cut to fit along the top of your basin or sink and half as deep
PVA (white) glue
mixing bowl
old household paintbrush
bradawl or other sharp implement
soft dark pencil
tile nippers
protective goggles
thin glazed ceramic household tiles, in 2 contrasting colours
flexible knife
rubber (latex) gloves
white cement-based tile adhesive
notched spreader or cloth pad
sandpaper
yacht varnish
screwdriver
4 domed mirror screws

1 Prime both sides of the plywood with diluted PVA (white) glue. Leave to dry, then score one side with a sharp implement.

2 Divide the scored side of the plywood into eight squares. Draw a motif into each square using the templates at the back of the book.

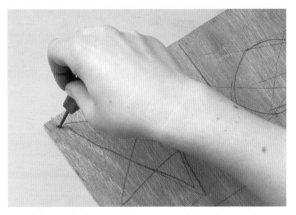

3 Make a hole in each corner of the plywood, using a bradawl. These will form the holes for the screws to fix the splashback to the wall.

4 Using tile nippers, and wearing goggles to protect your eyes, cut the tiles into random shapes. Here the motifs are picked out alternately in dark blue and pale yellow, with the other colour used as the background. Following your drawn designs, stick the tiles in place with PVA (white) glue over the pencil markings on each square. Position the tiles carefully around the holes made for hanging. When each square is glued into position, wipe off any excess glue with a soft pad, before it dries. Leave until completely dry, preferably overnight.

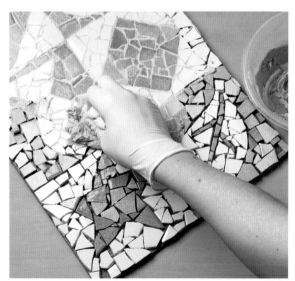

5 Wearing rubber (latex) gloves, mix the tile adhesive as recommended by the manufacturer. Wipe it over the surface of the mosaic with a notched spreader or cloth pad, smoothing around the edges with your fingers. Wipe off any excess adhesive and re-open the holes. Leave to dry overnight.

6 Carefully sand off any remaining dried adhesive on the surface of the mosaic. Paint the back of the plywood with yacht varnish to seal it and make it waterproof, and leave to dry for 1-2 hours. Fasten the splashback to the wall with mirror screws inserted through the four holes at each corner.

DAISY-COVERED TABLE

This wonderful table is literally strewn with daisies — green stems twine around the legs and a carpet of pretty white flowers spreads over the top. If the table has a rim, saw it off first to make the shape easier to mosaic.

YOU WILL NEED
small table
sandpaper
PVA (white) glue
mixing bowl
old household paintbrush
bradawl or other sharp implement
soft dark pencil
tile nippers
protective goggles
thin glazed ceramic household tiles: white,
yellow, green and pale pink
rubber (latex) gloves
cement-based tile adhesive
admix (see Materials)
flexible knife
hammer
heavy protective gloves
piece of sacking (heavy cloth)
notched spreader
sponge
dust mask
soft cloth

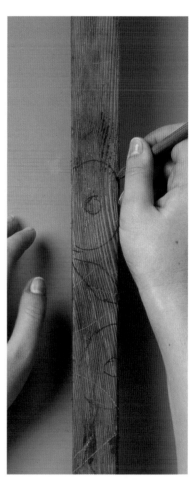

1 Remove any old wax, dirt, paint or varnish from the table, then sand and prime with diluted PVA (white) glue. Leave to dry, then score all the surfaces with a sharp implement.

2 Draw flowers and stems twisting around the legs and spreading over the tabletop, using the template at the back of the book, if desired. Take care when joining the legs to the table top.

3 Using tile nippers and wearing goggles, cut the yellow tiles into small squares, then nip off the corners to make circles for the centres of the flowers.

4 Cut the white tiles into small, equally-sized oblongs. Make these into petal shapes by nipping off the corners of each oblong.

5 Wearing rubber (latex) gloves, mix the tile adhesive and admix together. Using a flexible knife, spread over a pencilled flower outline. Press in a flower centre and petal – you may need to cut some petals on the legs in half. Complete all the flowers.

6 Spread a thin coat of the adhesive and admix mixture directly on to the table, along the pencil outlines of the stems and leaves. Cut the green tiles into appropriate stem and leaf shapes and press in place. Leave to dry overnight.

7 Using a hammer, and wearing goggles and heavy gloves for protection, break up the pink tiles. It is advisable to wrap each tile in a piece of sacking (heavy cloth) to prevent splintering and shattering.

8 Wearing rubber (latex) gloves and working on a small area at a time, spread tile adhesive and admix over the background areas. Press in the pink tile pieces to fit. Leave to dry overnight.

9 Wearing rubber (latex) gloves, grout the mosaic with tile adhesive. Use a notched spreader for the large flat areas. Wipe off the excess with a damp sponge and leave to dry overnight.

10 Wearing a dust mask, carefully sand the surface of the table to remove any lumps of dried adhesive still remaining. Wipe the table with a damp sponge if necessary, and polish with a soft cloth.

VALENTINE MIRROR

In this lovely hallway mirror, romantic red hearts and scrolling white lines are beautifully set off by the rich blue background, which sparkles with chunks of mirror glass. Choose the size and shape of the mirror to suit your wall space.

YOU WILL NEED

rectangle of 12 mm (½ in) thick plywood, cut to size required
PVA (white) glue
mixing bowl
old household paintbrush
bradawl or other sharp implement
hand drill
mirror plate, with keyhole opening
screwdriver
12 mm (½ in) screws
scissors
brown paper
masking tape
rectangle of mirror glass, cut to size required
ruler
soft dark pencil
cement-based tile adhesive
tile nippers
protective goggles
thin glazed ceramic household tiles: red, white and several rich shades of blue
rubber (latex) gloves
hammer
heavy protective gloves
mirror glass tiles
piece of sacking (heavy cloth)
notched spreader
dust mask
fine sandpaper

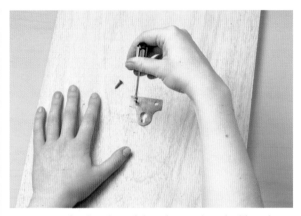

1 Prime both sides of the plywood with diluted PVA (white) glue and leave to dry. Score one side (the front) with a sharp implement. Turn the board over and make a dent in the centre, using a drill. Screw the mirror plate over the dent.

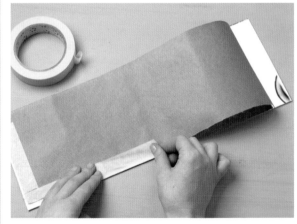

2 Cut a piece of brown paper to the size of the mirror and tape it round the edge, to protect the glass. Mark its position in the centre front of the board and stick in place with tile adhesive.

3 Draw a small heart in the centre of each border and scrolling lines to connect the four hearts. Use the template at the back of the book if desired.

4 Using tile nippers and wearing goggles, cut the blue and red tiles into small, irregular pieces. Cut the white tiles into regular-sized squares.

5 Mix the tile adhesive as recommended by the manufacturer. It is advisable to wear rubber (latex) gloves. Spread the adhesive over the pencilled heart shapes and press in the red tile pieces. Repeat for the white lines. Scrape off any excess adhesive and leave to dry overnight.

6 Using a hammer, and wearing goggles and rubber (latex) gloves to protect your eyes and hands, carefully break up the blue and mirror glass tiles into small pieces. It is advisable to wrap each tile in a piece of sacking (heavy cloth) before breaking up, to avoid the tile shattering or splintering.

7 Working on a small area at a time, and wearing rubber (latex) gloves, spread tile adhesive over the background areas then press in the blue and glass pieces. Leave to dry overnight.

8 Grout the mosaic with tile adhesive, wearing rubber (latex) gloves as before. Use a notched spreader to distribute the glue over the flat surface and your gloved fingers for the edges.

9 Wearing a dust mask, carefully sand off any lumps of remaining adhesive which may have dried on the surface of the mosaic, using fine sandpaper.

10 For a professional finish, rub tile adhesive into the back of the plywood board. Remove the protective brown paper from the mirror.

STAINED GLASS SCREEN

In this project the mosaic is laid on top of clear glass. Place the screen in front of a window by day or a glowing fire at night so that the light shines through.

YOU WILL NEED
mitre block
tape measure
hacksaw
3 pieces of 2.5 cm (1 in) x 3.5 cm (1½ in)
wood, each 206 cm (82½ in) long, with a
1 cm (½ in) rebate
wood glue
hammer
12 corner staples
dark pencil
hand drill
4 small hinges
screwdriver
screws
large sheet of paper
black marker pen
3 pieces of clear glass, each 70 x 25 cm
(28 in x 10 in)
indelible marker pen
glass cutter
protective goggles
7 pieces of coloured glass,
27 cm (10½ in) square
clear all-purpose adhesive
tile grout
universal black stain
rubber (latex) gloves
mixing bowl
old toothbrush
paint scraper
soft cloth
3 pieces of rectangular beading, each
2 m (78 in) long
panel pins (narrow-headed nails)
12 metal corner plates

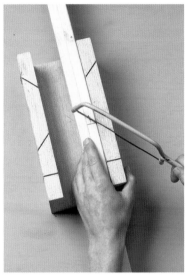

1 Using a mitre block and a hacksaw, cut six pieces of rebated wood 74 cm (29 in) long. Cut six more lengths of rebated wood each 29 cm (11½ in) long. These will form the wooden frame for the screen.

2 Lay the pieces of wood out on a flat surface to make three oblong frames. Glue the mitred ends together with wood glue, checking they are at right angles. Leave to dry, then hammer in a corner staple at each corner.

3 Place one frame on top of another, with the rebates facing outwards. With a pencil, mark the position of two hinges and their screwholes as shown. Using a hand drill, make a shallow guidehole for each screw, then screw in the hinges. Attach the third frame in the same way to form a three-piece screen.

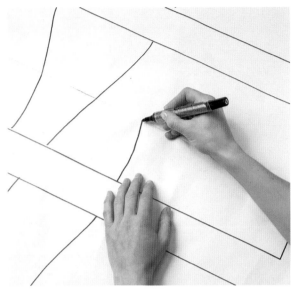

4 Place the three frames face down on a large sheet of paper. Using a marker pen, draw around the inner edge of each frame. Draw a simple design which flows in bands of colour from one frame to the next.

5 Place the pieces of clear glass over the paper drawing – the glass will be slightly larger. Using an indelible pen, trace your design on to the glass, taking care not to press too hard against it.

6 Using a glass cutter and wearing protective goggles, cut 12 right-angled triangles of coloured glass (see Techniques) for the corners of the screen. Reserve on one side. Cut the rest into random pieces.

7 Using clear adhesive, glue the coloured pieces on to the clear glass panels. Work on a section of your design at a time, following each band across to the other panels. Leave to dry for 2 hours.

8 Mix the tile grout with the black stain and rub over the surface of the mosaic – it is advisable to wear rubber (latex) gloves. Use a toothbrush to make sure all the gaps are filled. Leave to dry for 1 hour.

9 When completely dry, clean off the excess grout. Residual, stubborn grout can be carefully removed with a paint scraper. Finish removing any smaller areas of grout with a soft cloth.

10 Glue one of the reserved right-angled triangles of coloured glass over the corner of the frames, at the front. Repeat with the other triangles, on each corner of the frame.

11 Cut the beading into six 71 cm (28 in) lengths and six 23 cm (9 in) lengths. Place the glass panels in the frames, slot the beading behind them and fix with panel pins (narrow-headed nails).

12 Make shallow guideholes with a hand drill, then screw the corner plates to the back of each corner of the frame. Finally, polish the surface of the mosaic screen with a soft cloth.

SPIRAL VASE

Gently spiralling bands of mosaic look very elegant on a tall vase shape. Small chips of gold smalti give extra highlights.

YOU WILL NEED
tall vase
paintbrush (optional)
yacht varnish (optional)
piece of white chalk
hammer
protective goggles
rubber (latex) gloves
marble tile
piece of sacking (heavy cloth)
cement-based tile adhesive
mixing bowl
flexible knife
glazed ceramic household tiles: pale blue and royal blue
tile nippers
gold smalti (see Materials)
notched spreader or cloth pad
dust mask
sandpaper
soft cloth

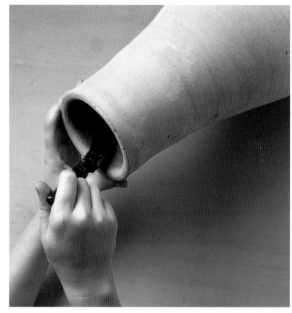

1 If your vase is unglazed, seal it by painting the inside top lip with yacht varnish.

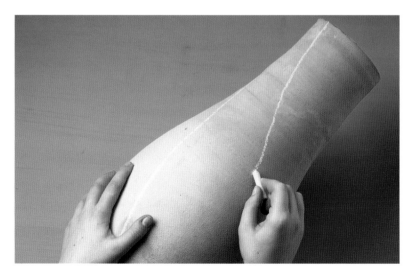

2 Using a piece of white chalk, draw lines spiralling gently from the rim of the vase to the base. Make sure you have an even number of bands and that they are regularly spaced.

3 Using a hammer, and wearing goggles and rubber (latex) gloves, break up the marble tile, wrapping it first in sacking (heavy cloth). Mix the tile adhesive according to the manufacturer's instructions. Using a flexible knife, spread a thin band around the top and bottom of the vase, press in the marble pieces and leave to dry overnight.

4 Using a hammer and sacking as before, and wearing the protective goggles, break up all the pale blue and royal blue tiles. Still wearing rubber (latex) gloves, spread tile adhesive over the vase, a band at a time, and press in the blue tesserae, alternating the two shades. Leave until completely dry, preferably overnight.

5 Wearing goggles, cut the gold smalti into small pieces with tile nippers. Using the knife, place blobs of adhesive in the larger gaps between the blue tesserae. Press in the gold smalti pieces at random over the blue spirals, checking that they are level with the rest of the tiles. Leave to dry overnight.

6 Using a notched spreader or cloth pad, and wearing rubber (latex) gloves, rub more tile adhesive over the mosaic, filling all the gaps. Wipe off the excess and leave to dry overnight. Wearing a dust mask, sand off any adhesive dried on the surface, then polish with a soft cloth.

CHINA RAIL

Make this useful kitchen rail out of old patterned china. Carry through the kitchen theme by using cups, plates and jars for the circular designs.

YOU WILL NEED
jigsaw
12 mm (½ in) thick MDF, 60 x 25 cm (24 x 10 in)
dust mask
sandpaper
PVA (white) glue
mixing bowl
old household paintbrush
dark pencil
60 cm (24 in) long metal rail, with struts
2 mirror plates
screws
screwdriver
plates, cups and jars, in different sizes
hammer
protective goggles
heavy protective gloves
old patterned crockery (china)
piece of sacking (heavy cloth)
tile nippers
rubber (latex) gloves
tile grout
old spoon
piece of cloth
notched spreader
soft cloth
S-shaped metal hooks

1 Using a jigsaw, cut the MDF so that it is 15 cm (6 in) high on either side, rising to a smooth curve in the centre. Wearing a dust mask, sand the edges until smooth. Prime both sides of the board with diluted PVA (white) glue.

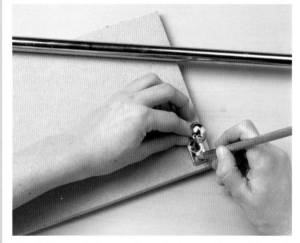

2 Using a dark pencil, mark the position of the rail fittings and screwholes clearly on the front of the board, one at either end.

33

3 Turn the board over and screw a mirror plate in the centre of each side edge. These will be used for hanging the rail to the wall.

4 Turn the board over again, to the front. Draw around upturned plates, cups and jars to create a design of circles in different sizes.

5 Using a hammer, and wearing goggles and rubber (latex) gloves, break up the old patterned crockery (china). It is advisable to wrap each piece in sacking (heavy cloth) first to prevent injuries.

6 Using tile nippers and wearing goggles, trim the fragments of crockery into neat squares, making the best use of the existing patterns on the crockery. Cut up all the crockery in this way.

7 Working from the outside top layer first, stick the tesserae to the board with PVA (white) glue, following the lines of your pencil design. Build up the pattern, leaving a space in between each tile for the grout to fill. You may find it easier to work from the outside pattern inwards. Avoid laying tesserae over the marked screwholes. Remove any excess glue with an old cloth as you work, and when the design is complete, leave to dry thoroughly, preferably overnight.

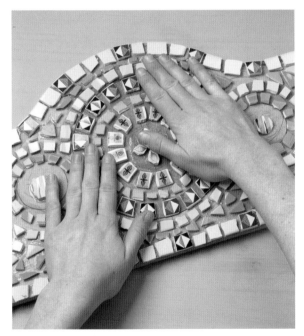

8 When dry, rub your hands over the surface of the mosaic to check for any loose tesserae. If any pieces have worked their way loose, glue these down again and leave to dry.

9 Wearing rubber (latex) gloves and using a notched spreader, spread tile grout over the surface of the mosaic, filling all the gaps between the tesserae. Leave to dry for 1 hour.

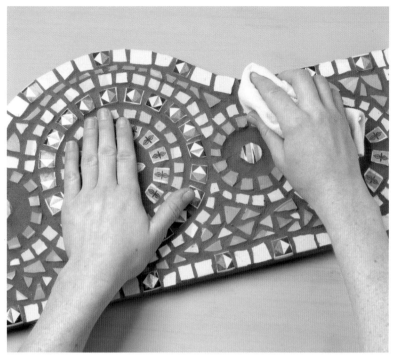

10 Polish the mosaic with a soft cloth, removing any grout which may have dried on the surface. Scrape off any stubborn grout with the back of an old spoon if necessary.

11 Wearing rubber (latex) gloves, smooth tile grout along all the edges of the board for a smooth finish. Leave to dry overnight and sand smooth.

12 Screw the rail and struts to the front of the board, then screw it firmly to the wall, using the mirror plates. Hang the S-shaped hooks on the rail.

DECORATIVE PANEL

A panelled piece of furniture is ideal for mosaic because it gives you a ready-made frame in which to work. This simple geometric design is made with pieces of old crockery (china).

YOU WILL NEED
piece of wooden furniture with a framed panel or panels
PVA (white) glue
mixing bowl
old household paintbrush
bradawl or other sharp implement
soft dark pencil
masking tape
tile nippers
protective goggles
old crockery (china)
cement-based tile adhesive
admix (see Materials)
rubber (latex) gloves
piece of old cloth
dust mask
fine sandpaper block
paint scraper
soft cloth, for polishing

1 Remove any varnish or polish from the areas of wood you wish to mosaic. Prime with diluted PVA (white) glue and leave to dry. Score the surface with a bradawl or sharp implement.

2 Draw a simple design on to the wood, or use one of the templates at the back of the book.

3 Stick masking tape around the raised edges of the panel(s) to protect the surrounding wood.

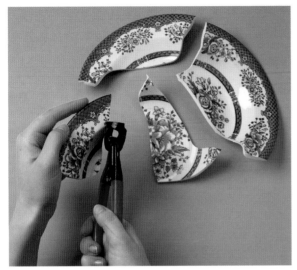

4 Using tile nippers and wearing goggles, cut the crockery (china) into small, random shapes. Sort the pieces into colours or shades of particular colours. Test out the colour scheme by positioning the pieces on to the design until you are satisfied.

5 Mix the tile adhesive with admix according to the manufacturer's instructions. Working on a small area at a time, spread the mixture over each area of the pencil design and press on the tesserae. It is advisable to wear rubber (latex) gloves. Leave to dry.

6 Wearing rubber (latex) gloves, grout the mosaic with more tile adhesive and admix mixture. The crockery (china) pieces will make an uneven surface, so use a piece of cloth to reach into all the gaps. Wipe off the excess then leave to dry overnight.

7 Wearing a dust mask, carefully sand off any residual tile adhesive which may have dried on the surface of the mosaic, using a fine sandpaper block. Use a paint scraper to reach stubborn or awkward areas such as those next to the wood.

8 When the residual grout is removed, carefully pull off the masking tape from around the edges of the mosaic panels.

9 Finally, remove any remaining dried grout from the mosaic panels and polish the surface with a soft cloth.

SLATE SHELF

This dramatic mosaic creates the invigorating effect of rocks sparkling with drops of water in a mountain stream. This project is quick to complete as it does not need to be grouted.

YOU WILL NEED

2 cm (¾ in) thick plywood, cut to fit over your basin or sink
bradawl or other sharp implement
PVA (white) glue
mixing bowl
old household paintbrush
hammer
protective goggles
rubber (latex) gloves
slate
piece of sacking (heavy cloth)
cement-based tile adhesive
teaspoon
universal black stain
flexible knife
pebbles
glass globules: blue, grey and white
silver smalti (see Materials)
tile nippers

1 Lightly score one side of the thick plywood with a bradawl or other sharp implement. Prime with diluted PVA (white) glue.

2 Using a hammer and wearing goggles, break the slate into large chunks. It is advisable to wrap the slate in sacking (heavy cloth) to prevent injury and wear rubber (latex) gloves.

3 Wearing rubber (latex) gloves, mix the tile adhesive with half a teaspoon of black cement stain to colour the glue. Add enough cold water to mix to a thick paste.

4 Using a flexible knife, spread the tile adhesive in a thick, even layer over the scored plywood shelf. Smooth it over the front to conceal the edge. Leave until thoroughly dry.

5 Arrange the broken slate, pebbles, glass globules and silver smalti on a flat surface next to the board, and arrange your design, making any adjustments until you are satisfied.

6 Transfer the design, piece by piece, to the board. Tap the slate with the side of tile nippers to settle it, but don't move any pieces once firmly positioned. Leave to dry overnight.

STAINED GLASS CANDLE-HOLDER

Squares of coloured glass cast beautiful patterns at night, when the candle is lit in a darkened room. Practise the glass-cutting technique first on scraps of clear glass.

YOU WILL NEED
pencil
ruler
graph paper
sheets of textured coloured glass
glass cutter
pliers
protective goggles
clear all-purpose adhesive
clear glass candle-holder
white tile grout
mixing bowl
flexible knife
rubber (latex) gloves
sponge or soft cloth

1 Using a pencil and ruler, draw a grid of 4 cm (1½ in) squares on graph paper.

2 Place each sheet of coloured glass over the grid. Following your drawn lines, score vertical lines with a glass cutter (see Techniques).

3 Using pliers and wearing goggles, snap the glass along the scored lines (see Techniques) into neat, evenly-sized pieces.

45

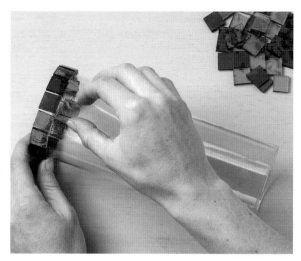

4 Place each strip of glass over the paper grid, score horizontal lines and snap off the squares, until you have enough squares to cover the candle-holder.

5 Stick the squares of glass in neat rows around the candle-holder with clear glue, alternating the colours, and leaving a tiny gap in between each tile.

6 Mix the tile grout as recommended by the manufacturer. Using a flexible knife, spread over the surface of the candle-holder, filling all the gaps between the squares. It is advisable to wear rubber (latex) gloves. Rub the excess grout off the surface with a damp sponge or soft cloth. Leave to dry completely before using.

COSMIC CLOCK

In this vivid mosaic, it is important that the tesserae are accurately shaped, with no gaps between them. They are left ungrouted so that tile adhesive dust will not disturb the workings of the clock. Practise first on less precise projects.

YOU WILL NEED

strip of plywood, 2 mm (¹⁄₁₂ in) thicker than the circle of wood and 130 cm (52 in) long
circle of wood, 40 cm (16 in) diameter
hammer
tacks
black paint
paintbrush
scissors
brown paper
hand drill
clock mechanism and hands
stick of charcoal or black marker pen
vitreous glass mosaic tesserae
water-soluble glue and brush
tile nippers
protective goggles
quick-drying cement-based tile adhesive
admix (see Materials)
mixing bowl
fine-toothed spreader
rubber (latex) gloves
piece of flat wood, for smoothing mosaic
craft knife
sponge
soft cloth
double-sided tape
picture hook

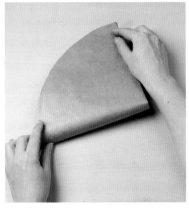

1 Position the strip of plywood around the circumference of the circle of wood and, using a hammer and tacks, cover the edge of the circle to make a neat rim. Paint the rim black and leave to dry. Cut a circular piece of brown paper to fit inside the rim. Fold the paper in quarters to find the centre and make a small hole.

2 Place the paper over the circle of wood and mark the centre through the hole on to the wood. Remove the paper and then drill a hole through the centre of the wood, large enough for the spindle of the clock mechanism to rotate freely.

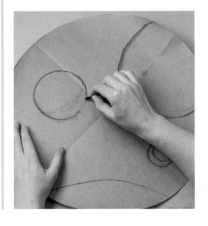

3 Draw a cosmic design on the brown paper circle, using charcoal or marker pen. (Charcoal is easier to correct.)

▶

4 Stick the glass tesserae face down on the paper, using water-soluble glue. Place them as close together as possible, without any gaps in between. Using tile nippers and wearing goggles, cut them to fit around the curves in your design.

5 Mix the tile adhesive with latex admix to form a thick paste. Using a fine-toothed spreader, spread this over the whole of the board, making sure you cover right up to the edge. It is advisable to wear rubber (latex) gloves for this.

6 Lower the mosaic into the adhesive and press flat. Smooth over the paper with a piece of flat wood, using small, circular movements. Leave for 20 minutes, then dampen the paper and gently pull it away from the mosaic. Scrape away any adhesive which has come through the tesserae with a craft knife. Leave to dry for at least 2 hours or until completely dry.

7 Carefully wipe any remaining glue from the surface of the mosaic with a damp sponge and polish with a soft cloth. Using double-sided tape, attach the clock mechanism to the back of the board. Insert the spindle through the hole in the centre and fit on the hands. Fit a picture hook to the back of the clock at the top, for fixing to the wall.

LEMON TREE FLOOR

This lovely design is inspired by the cool tiled floors in Mediterranean countries. The mosaic is covered with a sheet of adhesive-backed plastic and lowered on to the floor in sections.

YOU WILL NEED
scissors
large sheet of white paper
coloured paper
black marker pen
tile cutter
glazed ceramic household tiles: various shades of yellow, green and grey
tile nippers
protective goggles
old plain and patterned crockery (china)
black mosaic tiles
glazed white tiles
large sheet of adhesive-backed plastic
craft knife
cement-based tile adhesive
mixing bowl
notched spreader
rubber (latex) gloves

1 Use the templates at the back of the book to create lemon and leaf shapes to cover the area of floor you wish to mosaic.

2 Cut large lemon and leaf shapes out of coloured paper and arrange on the large sheet of white paper. When you are happy with the design, draw in details such as stems and a decorative border around the edge of the design, using a marker pen.

3 Using a tile cutter, score all the large coloured household tiles down the centre. You may need to practise on some spares to get a straight line.

4 Break each tile into neat halves by applying equal pressure on either side of the scored line with the tile cutter. This will result in a clean break.

5 Using tile nippers and wearing goggles, cut these tile pieces into small, equal-sized shapes. Cut up the crockery (china) in the same way. Also cut up some of the black mosaic tiles, enough to outline each lemon, again into equally-sized pieces.

6 Following your paper design, arrange the pieces on a flat surface. To make the lemons appear three-dimensional, place the darker shades on one side. Outline each shape with black mosaic tiles and extend to make a stem.

7 Using tile nippers and wearing goggles, cut the white tiles into random shapes. Fill in the background with a mosaic of large and small pieces.

8 Finish with a border. This undulating border is made of square, yellow-toned tesserae, outlined with rectangular black tiles.

9 Peel the backing paper off the adhesive-backed plastic and lay it carefully over the loose mosaic. You may have to work in sections.

10 Smooth your hands over the plastic to make sure it has adhered to all the tesserae and that any air bubbles are eliminated.

11 Using a craft knife, cut through the plastic to separate the mosaic into manageable sections.

12 Mix the tile adhesive according to the manufacturer's instructions and spread over the floor area, using a notched spreader. Lower the mosaic carefully into the tile adhesive, section by section. It is advisable to wear rubber (latex) gloves at this stage. Press down and leave to dry overnight. Peel off the plastic then grout the mosaic with more tile adhesive (see Techniques).

COUNTRY COTTAGE TRAY

This story-book picture is made in vitreous glass tiles, which are waterproof and heatproof.
The semi-indirect method of mosaic helps to keep the surface smooth and flat.

YOU WILL NEED
scissors
brown paper
wooden tray
pencil
tile nippers
protective goggles
vitreous glass mosaic tiles
water-soluble glue
white spirit
PVA (white) glue
mixing bowl
old household paintbrush
bradawl or other sharp instrument
masking tape
cement-based tile adhesive
notched spreader
rubber (latex) gloves
sponge and soft cloth

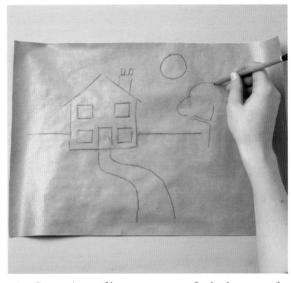

1 Cut a piece of brown paper to fit the bottom of the tray. Draw a simple picture in pencil or trace the template at the back of the book.

2 Plan out the colour scheme for the picture and, using tile nippers and wearing goggles, cut each tile into quarters. You may like to position the tiles on to the paper to check your design before going any further. Once you are satisfied with the design, apply water-soluble glue to the paper in small areas, and stick the tiles face down. Take care to obscure any pencil marks. Trim the tiles to fit if necessary. ▶

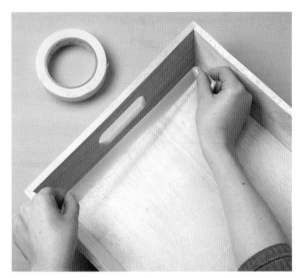

3 Prepare the bottom of the tray by removing any varnish or polish with white spirit. Prime with diluted PVA (white) glue, leave to dry, then score with a sharp instrument such as a bradawl. Protect the sides of the tray with masking tape.

4 Mix the tile adhesive according to the manufacturer's instructions. Spread an even layer over the bottom of the tray, using a notched spreader. Cover the tray completely and spread well into the corners. It is advisable to wear rubber (latex) gloves.

5 Place the mosaic carefully in the freshly applied tile adhesive, paper side up. Press down firmly over the whole surface, then leave for 30 minutes. Moisten the paper with a damp sponge and peel off. Leave the tile adhesive to dry overnight.

6 Some parts of the mosaic may need to be grouted with extra tile adhesive (see Techniques). Leave to dry, then clean off any adhesive which may have dried on the surface with a sponge. Remove the masking tape and polish the mosaic with a soft cloth.

FLORAL LAMP BASE

A breeze (concrete) block makes a safe, solid base for a large floor lamp. Cover it in a chunky floral design made of floor tiles, marble and tiny pieces of mirror, set into the gaps to catch the light from the lamp.

YOU WILL NEED
breeze (concrete) block
ruler
soft pencil
drill, with a long bit (at least half the length of the block)
chisel
lamp flex (cord)
hollow metal rod, with a thread cut into it
rubber (latex) gloves
cement-based tile adhesive
piece of chalk
protective goggles
rubber (latex) gloves
ceramic floor tiles, in yellow and one other colour
piece of sacking (heavy cloth)
hammer
flexible knife
white marble tiles
tile nippers
mirror glass
notched spreader
sponge
dust mask
sandpaper
lamp fittings
short piece of copper pipe
plug
screwdriver
soft cloth

1 On one end of the breeze (concrete) block, mark diagonal lines to find the centre. Drill a hole right through the centre, turning the block over if necessary to drill from the other end.

2 On one end, use a chisel to cut a deep groove to contain the flex (cord), from the centre hole to one edge. This will be the bottom of the lamp base. ▶

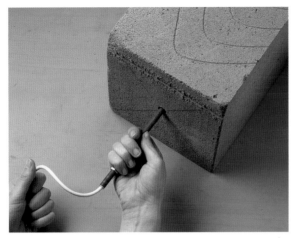

3 Thread the flex (cord) through the centre hole, leaving a long length at the bottom. At the top, pass it through the metal rod as shown. Lay the block on its side and pull the flex (cord) through the groove. Wearing rubber (latex) gloves, mix some tile adhesive according to the manufacturer's instructions, and fill in the groove to secure the flex (cord). Leave to dry.

4 Using a piece of chalk, draw a large, simple flower design on the sides of the breeze (concrete) block, either free-hand or tracing the template from the back of the book. Exclude the bottom of the block. Plan out the colour scheme for your petals, keeping the yellow for the flower centres and white for the background.

5 Wearing goggles and heavy gloves, wrap each floor tile in sacking (heavy cloth) and break it up into pieces with a hammer. Using a flexible knife and still wearing rubber (latex) gloves, spread tile adhesive over each flower shape. Press the yellow tesserae into the adhesive and build up the flower centres. Continue with the petals until they are all covered.

6 Wearing goggles, wrap each white marble tile in sacking (heavy cloth) and break it into pieces with the hammer. Working on a small area at a time, and wearing rubber (latex) gloves, spread tile adhesive over the background and press in the marble pieces. Don't worry if your pieces don't butt up to each other. Leave to dry overnight.

7 Using tile nippers and wearing goggles, cut the mirror glass into small fragments. Wearing rubber (latex) gloves, insert blobs of tile adhesive in the larger gaps between the tesserae. Wearing heavy gloves, push in the mirror fragments, checking they are level with the rest. Continue inserting mirrored pieces over the base until covered. Leave to dry overnight.

8 Wearing rubber (latex) gloves, grout the lamp base by scraping tile adhesive over the surface with a notched spreader. This will bind all the pieces of tesserae together firmly. Use your gloved fingers to smooth it right into the fissures, and along the sides of the block. Wipe off the excess tile adhesive with a damp sponge and leave to dry overnight.

9 Wearing a dust mask, sand off any adhesive which may have dried on the surface.

10 Attach the lamp fittings to the threaded metal rod, then conceal the rod inside the copper pipe. Attach a suitable plug to the bottom end of the flex (cord). Finally, polish the base with a soft cloth.

STAR TABLE TOP

This traditional design uses the colours seen in ancient Roman mosaics to create a table top suitable for a simple metal base. Unglazed tiles are much easier than glazed tiles to cut and shape for a precise design such as this.

YOU WILL NEED
2 cm (¾ in) thick plywood, cut to fit metal table base
PVA (white) glue
mixing bowl
old household paintbrush
bradawl or other sharp implement
pair of compasses (compass)
pencil
ruler
black marker pen (optional)
tile nippers
protective goggles
unglazed ceramic mosaic tiles: white, beige, black and terracotta
fine artist's paintbrush, for glue
cement-based tile adhesive
rubber (latex) gloves
sponge
sandpaper
dust mask
soft cloth

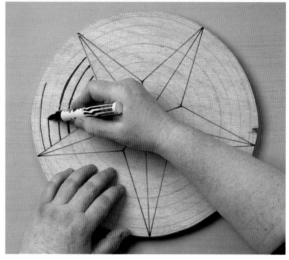

1 Prime one side of the plywood with diluted PVA (white) glue and leave to dry. Score with a bradawl. Using a pair of compasses (compass), draw circles 1 cm (½ in) apart, from the centre. Draw the star on top, or use the template from the back of the book. If you wish, go over the design in marker pen.

2 Using tile nippers and wearing goggles, cut the white tiles into neat quarters. Apply PVA (white) glue to the base in small sections, using a fine paintbrush. Stick the tesserae on to alternate sections of the star. Keep the rows straight and the gaps between the tesserae even and to a minimum. Trim the tesserae as necessary to fit. Continue laying the tesserae until all the white sections are complete. ▶

3 Cut up the beige tiles into neat quarters and fill in the other sections of the star in the same way as the white tiles in step 2.

4 Wearing goggles, cut the black tiles into neat quarters and glue around the edge of the plywood. Leave until completely dry.

5 Glue a row of black quarter-tiles around the outer edge of the table top. Wearing goggles, cut some white quarter-tiles in half and glue inside the black circle, keeping the gaps to a minimum. Cut the terracotta tiles into quarters.

6 Using your drawn lines as a guide, fill in the rest of the background with alternating bands of colour. Lay out the tesserae first before you glue them in place. Leave to dry overnight, then grout with tile adhesive and clean the surface (see Techniques).

TRINKET BOX

This delicate mosaic is made entirely from old cups and plates. Plain white pieces are used for the borders around the squares, which contain individual flowers made of patterned china.

YOU WILL NEED
wooden box
PVA (white) glue
mixing bowl
old household paintbrush
bradawl or other sharp instrument
soft dark pencil
tile nippers
protective goggles
old china: white and patterned
cement-based tile adhesive
admix
flexible knife
rubber (latex) gloves
cloth or sponge
paint scraper
soft cloth, for polishing

1 Prime the top and sides of the wooden box with diluted PVA (white) glue. Leave to dry, then score at random with a bradawl or other sharp implement.

2 Using a soft pencil, and the template at the back of the book, draw a grid on the box. Draw a flower in each square, with a large flower in the centre.

3 Using tile nippers and wearing goggles, cut white pieces of china into small squares. Mix the tile adhesive with admix. Using a flexible knife, spread this along the grid lines, a small area at a time.

4 Press the white tesserae into the adhesive in neat, close-fitting rows – it is advisable to wear rubber (latex) gloves. Cover all the grid lines on the top and sides of the box. Leave to dry overnight.

5 Wearing goggles and using tile nippers, cut out small patterned pieces from the china. Sort them into colours. Position the tesserae on the box and plan out the colour scheme.

6 Wearing rubber (latex) gloves, spread the tile adhesive and admix over each square of the top and sides in turn. Press in the tesserae to make each flower and the background. Leave to dry.

7 Still wearing rubber (latex) gloves, spread tile adhesive all over the surface of the mosaic, getting right into the crevices. Wipe off any excess adhesive with a damp cloth or sponge.

8 Using a flexible knife, smooth the tile adhesive around the hinges and clasp, if there is one. Remove any excess adhesive immediately with a cloth before it dries. Leave to dry.

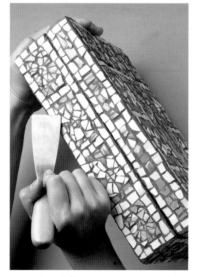

9 Carefully scrape off any tile adhesive, which may have dried on the surface of the mosaic, with a paint scraper. Take care not to scratch the surface of the tiles.

10 When all the excess grout has been removed, polish the surface of the box with a soft cloth, rubbing each tile fragment to a high shine.

FUNKY FRUIT BOWL

In this unusual modern design, the coloured grout is for once a major feature, with large gaps left to show it off. The tesserae appear as separate decorative elements, rather than parts of a whole.

YOU WILL NEED
soft dark pencil
terracotta bowl
tile nippers
protective goggles
vitreous glass mosaic tiles: yellow, turquoise and white
PVA (white) glue
mixing bowl
fine artist's paintbrush, for glue
white glazed ceramic household tiles
matt coloured glass nuggets
powdered fabric dye
flexible knife
spoon
white tile grout
rubber (latex) gloves
notched spreader
soft cloth

1 Using a soft pencil, draw spirals on the outside of the bowl, as shown. Mark a row of triangles along the edges of each spiral.

2 Using tile nippers and wearing goggles, cut the glass tiles into small, equal-sized triangles, to fit the triangles drawn on the bowl.

3 Place a small blob of PVA (white) glue on each pencilled triangle, then press on a glass triangle. Hold the tesserae in place until they stick.

4 Using tile nippers and wearing goggles to protect your eyes, cut the white ceramic tiles into large triangles of equal size.

5 Apply a thick layer of glue over the inside of the bowl and over the back of each triangle. Press the triangles in place, leaving large gaps between them.

6 Dot blobs of glue at regular intervals around the rim of the bowl and press in the glass nuggets. Leave to dry overnight.

7 Mix the fabric dye with water. You can choose any of the many colours available. Bright primary colours will work well with this design.

▶

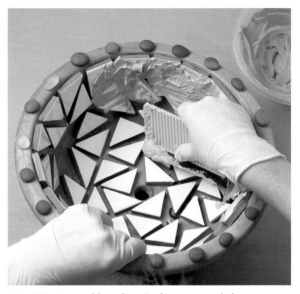

8 Gradually add the dye to the white tile grout powder, a spoonful at a time, and mix thoroughly. The final colour of the grout will be slightly lighter than the original shade.

9 Wearing rubber (latex) gloves, spread the coloured grout over the entire bowl, evening out the surface. Gently smooth over the bowl with gloved hands. Leave to dry for 1 hour.

10 Polish the surface of the bowl with a soft cloth, removing the extra tile grout.

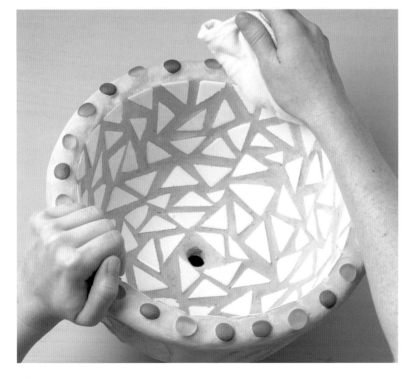

TREE OF LIFE WALL PANEL

This decorative picture is created using handpainted Mexican tiles, which are now widely available. Blue-and-white patterned tesserae make a lively background and the terracotta tree trunk is simply the unglazed back of the tiles.

YOU WILL NEED

2 cm (¾ in) thick plywood, cut to the size required – adjust your measurements to fit a row of whole border tiles in each direction

small, handpainted glazed ceramic tiles, for the border

tape measure

pencil

hand drill

mirror plate

screwdriver

12 mm (½ in) screws

PVA (white) glue

mixing bowl

old household paintbrush

bradawl or other sharp implement

soft dark pencil

tile nippers

protective goggles

plain glazed ceramic tiles: various shades of green and beige

blue-and-white handpainted glazed ceramic tiles

soft brush

cement-based tile adhesive

plant spray

rubber (latex) gloves

cloth

soft cloth

1 On the back of the plywood, mark a point halfway across the width and a third from the top. Drill a rebate to fit under the keyhole of the mirror plate. Screw the mirror plate in place.

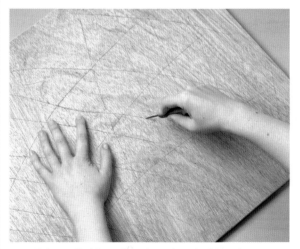

2 Prime all sides of the board with diluted PVA (white) glue. Leave to dry, then score the front with a bradawl or other sharp implement. ▶

3 Measure the border tiles and draw a frame of this size on the front of the board. Draw a simple tree or trace the template from the back of the book.

4 Using PVA (white) glue, cover the border of the board with glue and stick the border tiles in place, positioned closely together.

5 Using tile nippers and wearing goggles, cut the blue-and-white tiles into small irregular shapes. Glue in place to make up the background sky. For the tree trunk, cut the beige tiles in the same way. Place these face down on the board, then prime them with diluted glue. Cut and glue into position the beige tiles for the earth. Leave to dry overnight.

6 Brush dry tile adhesive over the panel, filling all the gaps between the tesserae, then spray with water until the adhesive is saturated. Leave to dry, and repeat if necessary. Wearing rubber (latex) gloves, rub the adhesive into the corners and crevices. Remove any excess adhesive with a cloth. Leave to dry overnight, then polish with a soft cloth.

BLACK-AND-WHITE FLOOR

No artistic skills are required for this stunning mosaic, as the picture is simply an old etching enlarged on a photocopier. The tesserae are glued on to fibreglass mesh, then lowered into position on the floor.

YOU WILL NEED
black-and-white image
clear plastic film (wrap)
masking tape
fibreglass mesh
tile nippers
protective goggles
unglazed mosaic ceramic tiles: black and white
PVA (white) glue
mixing bowl
fine artist's paintbrush, for glue
craft knife
cement-based tile adhesive
rubber (latex) gloves
notched spreader
flat wooden board
hammer
soft cloth

1 Decide on the image you wish to use: you may wish to build up a picture from various elements. Enlarge on a photocopier to the required size.

2 Working on a large work surface, cover the photocopy with clear plastic film (wrap) and secure the edges with masking tape. If your picture is built up of more than one image, repeat this process for all sections. ▶

3 Position a piece of fibreglass mesh over the plastic film (wrap) and tape down to the work surface with masking tape. Using tile nippers and wearing goggles, cut the tiles into quarters.

4 Beginning with the main features such as this boat, glue the tesserae to the fibreglass mesh using a fine paintbrush. Build up the picture, using the light and shade of the photocopy as a guide.

5 Outline the panel with a geometric border in black and white, cutting some of the tesserae in half to make triangular shapes.

6 Fill in the background of the design, simplifying and accentuating the black and white areas, until the photocopy is completely covered. Leave to dry.

7 Using a craft knife, cut through the mesh and plastic, chopping the mosaic into manageable sections. You may find it helpful to cut around the boat shape as shown.

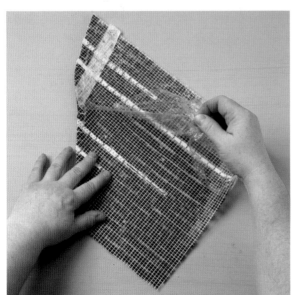

8 Turn the sections over and peel off the plastic. Using the craft knife, pierce any holes in the mesh that are clogged with glue.

9 Mix the adhesive according to the manufacturer's instructions. Wearing rubber (latex) gloves, spread over the bathroom floor, using a notched spreader. ▶

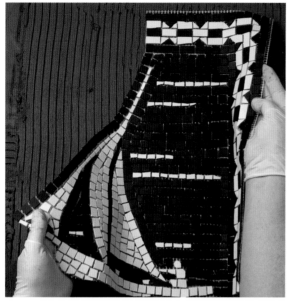

10 Carefully lay each section of the mosaic on the tile adhesive, mesh side down.

11 Place a flat board over each part of the mosaic and tap with a hammer to make sure the tesserae are firmly embedded into the adhesive. Leave to dry overnight, then grout with more tile adhesive (see Techniques). Polish with a soft cloth.

MATERIALS

The main materials used in mosaic are the individual pieces, the tesserae, which can be ceramic, glass, china or any other solid material. The other important material to consider is the base, which should be rigid and suitable for indoor or outdoor use, without warping or expanding.

ADHESIVES

As well as cement-based tile adhesive (see below), there are several other ways to attach tesserae. For a wood base, you can also use PVA (white) glue. For a glass base, use a silicone-based or clear, all-purpose adhesive; to stick glass to metal, use epoxy resin. PVA (white) glue is also used to prime a wooden base, to make a suitable surface for the mosaic to adhere to. The base should be scored with a craft knife before glue is applied (see Techniques).

ADMIX

This is a specialist material available from most craft stores, sold under a variety of commercial names. It is used to add to tile adhesive for projects which require extra adhesion and flexibility.

CEMENT-BASED TILE ADHESIVE

This is the most common way of securing ceramic tesserae to a wooden base. You can make your own cement mortar, using 3 parts builder's sand to 1 part cement, mixed with enough water to make it pliable. The same tile adhesive is also often used to grout between the tesserae once the design is complete. Cement-based tile adhesive can be coloured with dye, for decorative effect.

CROCKERY (CHINA)

Old household china makes unusual and interesting tesserae, especially if you select the plain and patterned pieces carefully. It creates an uneven surface, so is suitable for decorative projects rather than flat, functional surfaces such as a table top. It should be broken up using a hammer and heavy sacking (see Techniques).

GROUT

Mosaics are often grouted with the same tile adhesive as is used to secure the tesserae to the base. Specialist grouts are also available; they are smoother and come in a variety of colours.

MARBLE

Marble can be bought pre-cut into small squares; to cut it accurately yourself you need specialist tools, as it is extremely hard. You can break it into irregular shapes using a hammer (see Techniques).

MEXICAN TILES

Handpainted Mexican tiles are now widely available from craft specialist stores. They are excellent for borders and can be broken into smaller shapes in the usual way. They are quite small and thick, and are available in plain colours, as well as geometric patterns and individual motifs.

MIRROR GLASS

Shards of mirror glass add a reflective sparkle to a mosaic, and are often used as decorative details. Mirror glass can be cut with tile nippers, glass cutters, or broken with a hammer (see Techniques).

BROWN PAPER

Brown paper is used as the backing for mosaics created by the semi-indirect method (see Techniques). It is advisable to use the heaviest paper possible.

SHELLAC

This is sometimes used for sealing the finished mosaic. It provides a waterproof coating, so is ideal for mosaics designed for outside.

SMALTI

This is opaque glass cut into regular chunks. It is made by firing glass with oxides, metals and powdered marble. It has a softly reflective surface and is available in a wide range of colours. Gold and silver smalti are made by sandwiching gold and silver leaf in transparent coloured glass. Gold or silver smalti is often used to provide reflective details within a mosaic made with vitreous glass.

TESSERAE

This is the term for any small pieces of ceramic, glass or other material that make up a mosaic.

1 glass smalti 2 broken mirror tiles 3 vitreous glass tesserae 4 broken tiles 5 gold-leaf smalti 6 broken crockery (china)
7 powdered cement 8 epoxy resin 9 brown paper 10 paper glue 11 powdered tile grout 12 PVA (white) glue 13 shellac

TILES

Ceramic tiles are available in a range of colours and textures, glazed or unglazed. Ordinary household tiles can be cut to size using a hammer, or tile nippers for accurate or precise shapes (see Techniques). Unglazed tiles are easier to cut and shape.

VITREOUS GLASS TESSERAE

These are manufactured glass squares which are corrugated on the back to accommodate tile adhesive. The range of colours is not as large as smalti, but they are less expensive and easier to cut. Vitreous glass is the most popular material for making mosaics. It is very hardwearing and perfect for mosaic projects designed to be displayed outdoors.

EQUIPMENT

Many of the tools needed to do mosaics are ordinary household equipment; the rest can be purchased in a good hardware store. A pair of tile nippers is the main piece of specialist equipment you will need.

BRADAWL
This is used to score a primed wooden surface, creating a good base for the mosaic to adhere to. A craft knife is equally effective.

BRUSHES
Used to prime surfaces with diluted PVA (white) glue. A fine artist's paintbrush is used to apply glue to small tesserae. If you are using powdered grout, use a soft brush and brush off the excess.

CHALK
Chalk shows up clearly and is easy to erase.

CLAMPS OR BENCH VICE
These are needed to cut out the wooden base for projects such as a shelf or wall rack.

CLOTH
For cleaning and polishing.

CRAFT KNIFE
This is especially useful for mosaics done by the indirect or semi-indirect method, to cut the design into manageable sections.

DRILL
A hand drill is needed for hanging projects on the wall.

DUST MASK
It is recommended to wear a dust mask when you are sanding grout from the finished mosaic.

FLEXIBLE KNIFE
A palette knife or other flexible knife is useful for spreading tile adhesive on to complex designs.

GLASS CUTTER
Used to cut or score glass tesserae.

GLOVES
Rubber (latex) gloves should be worn whenever handling tile adhesive or grout. Heavy work gloves should be worn when you are smashing tiles with a hammer or working with glass fragments.

JIGSAW
Useful template for cutting shapes in wood.

HAMMER
This is useful for breaking up tiles. A hammer is also sometimes used to tap large pieces into place.

MARKER PEN
This is useful to draw the initial design as it will show up clearly.

MASKING TAPE
Used to mask off areas.

NAILBRUSH
Useful for removing grout from the surface of a mosaic.

MIXING BOWL
A selection of old kitchen bowls is useful for mixing tile adhesive and grout, and also for glue and dye.

PAINT SCRAPER
This is used to remove awkward pieces of dried tile adhesive or grout from the surface of a completed mosaic.

PENCIL
A dark pencil is best for drawing designs as it shows up well and can be erased if you make a mistake.

PLASTIC SPRAY BOTTLE
Used to saturate adhesive when grouting with dry adhesive.

PLIERS
These are used to snap a piece of glass in two after scoring it with a glass cutter (see Techniques).

PROTECTIVE GOGGLES
Wear safety goggles when you cut tiles with tile nippers, or smashing them with a hammer.

RULER
This is needed to measure smaller designs that require accuracy.

SACKING (HEAVY CLOTH)
Used when breaking up tiles to eliminate dangerous fragments.

SANDPAPER
Use coarse sandpaper to prepare wood. To clean the surface of finished mosaics, use fine-grade sandpaper and wear a dust mask.

SAW
Cut basic shapes such as shelves with a hacksaw.

SCISSORS
Useful for cutting paper, masking tape, etc.

SET SQUARE (T-SQUARE)
This will help you measure accurate right angles.

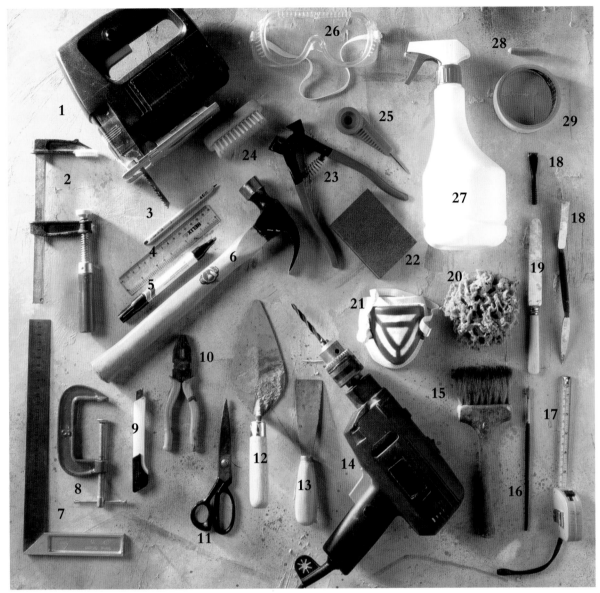

1 jigsaw 2 vice 3 pencil 4 ruler 5 marker pen 6 hammer 7 right-angled ruler 8 clamp 9 craft knife 10 pliers 11 scissors 12 trowel 13 spatula 14 drill 15 soft brush 16 paintbrush 17 tape measure 18 spreader 19 flexible knife 20 sponge 21 dust mask 22 sandpaper 23 tile nippers 24 nailbrush 25 bradawl 26 goggles 27 plastic spray bottle 28 chalk 29 masking tape

SPATULA
Used for spreading glue or grout.

SPONGE
For cleaning and polishing finished pieces. It is also used to soak off backing paper.

SPREADER
Used to spread adhesive and to apply grout in between tesserae.

TAPE MEASURE
Use a metal tape measure to mark out precise designs.

TILE NIPPERS
These are invaluable for cutting shaped tiles, especially curves.

TROWEL
A metal trowel can be used instead of a spreader or flexible knife.

TECHNIQUES

*There are various ways of cutting different materials such as ceramic and glass to make tesserae.
There are also different methods of laying mosaic. Always wear protective gloves and goggles as
specified in the projects.*

DIRECT METHOD

This is a popular mosaic-laying
technique, in which the tesserae
are stuck, face up, on to the base
and grouted into place. On an
three-dimensional object or
uneven surface this may be the
only suitable method.

1 Cover the base with adhesive.
Press the tesserae into it,
cover with grout, dry, then clean.

2 If you are following a design
drawn on the base as a guide,
apply a thin layer of tile adhesive
to each individual tesserae and
stick in to place. This way the
design will not be obscured.

3 If the tesserae are reflective,
such as mirror glass or gold
or silver smalti, you can place
them at slightly different angles
on a three-dimensional surface,
to catch the light.

SEMI-INDIRECT METHOD

This is a combination of the direct
and indirect methods. The tesserae
are glued to the design off-site,
but are then set into the tile
adhesive in the final position.

1 Draw a design on to brown
paper. Stick the tesserae face
down on to the paper.

2 Spread tile adhesive over the
final position for the mosaic.
Press the mosaic into the adhesive,
paper side up. Leave to dry for at
least 24 hours, protecting it from
rain if it is outdoors.

3 Dampen the paper with a wet
sponge and peel it off. Grout
and clean the mosaic. (See
Techniques).

INDIRECT METHOD

This technique originated as a way of making large mosaics off-site so that they could be transported ready-made. The design was divided into manageable sections which were fitted together on-site. Vitreous glass tesserae are ideal for this as they are the same colour front and back.

1 Make a wooden frame to the size required, securing the corners with 2.5 cm (1 in) screws. Make a brown paper template of the inside of the frame. Draw a design on the paper, leaving a 5 mm (¼ in) margin all around. Grease the inside of the frame with petroleum jelly.

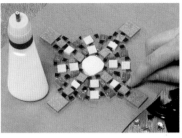

2 Cut the tesserae to the required size and shape. Using water-soluble adhesive, glue them face down on the paper, following the design. Leave to dry.

3 Place the frame carefully over the mosaic. Sprinkle dry sand over the mosaic, using a soft brush to spread it into the crevices between the tesserae. On a board, mix 3 parts sand with 1 part cement. Make a well in the centre, add water and mix with a trowel until you have a firm consistency. Gradually add more water, if necessary, until the mortar is pliable but not runny.

4 Half-fill the frame with mortar, pressing it into the corners. Cut a square of chicken wire a little smaller than the frame. Place it on top of the mortar so that the wire does not touch the frame. Fill the rest of the frame with mortar, then smooth the surface. Cover with damp newspaper, then heavy plastic sheeting, and leave to dry thoroughly, for 5-6 days.

5 Turn over the frame. Dampen the paper with a wet sponge and peel it off. Loosen the screws and remove the mosaic. Grout and clean the mosaic (see below).

MIX LIQUID LATEX INTO GROUT - extra Waterproofing.

CUTTING TESSERAE

1 The most flexible method is to use tile nippers, which are very simple to operate. Hold a tesserae between the tips of the nippers, squeeze the handles together, and it should break in two along the line of impact. To cut a specific shape such as a circle, nibble at the edges.

2 Use a hammer to break up larger pieces such as household tiles and crockery (china), where regular shapes are not required. Always wear protective goggles. It is also advisable to wrap each tile, plate, etc in a piece of sacking (heavy cloth) to prevent flying shards.

CLEANING FINISHED WORK

Try to remove most of the excess grout while it is still wet. Ready-made grout can be scrubbed off with a stiff-bristled brush, such as an old nailbrush, then polished with a soft cloth. Cement-based tile adhesive and mortar are harder to remove, and you will probably need to use sandpaper.

CUTTING GLASS

It is a good idea to practise this technique on scraps of clear glass before using a glass cutter on expensive coloured glass. It is advisable to wear protective gloves.

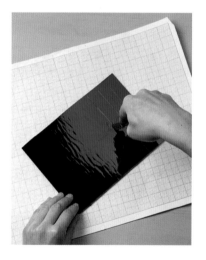

1 Hold the glass cutter in your palm and rest your index finger along the top. The cutter should be at an angle of 90 degrees to the glass.

2 Applying firm, even pressure, score a line across the glass in one movement, without a break. You can push the cutter away from you or pull it towards you. Don't score over the same line; if you make a mistake, try again on another part of the glass.

3 Hold the scored piece of glass in one hand. With your working hand, position pliers along the scored line and grip firmly. Angle the tip of the pliers up and pull down. The glass should break cleanly in two along the scored line.

GROUTING

Mosaics are grouted to give them extra strength and a smoother finish. Grout binds the tesserae together. Coloured grout is often used to unify the design. This can either be purchased as ready-made powder, or you can add ordinary clothes dye to plain grout. Some mosaics, for example smalti designs, are left ungrouted to give a more expressive effect. In these pieces the tesserae must be cut extremely precisely and positioned very closely together on to the base.

1 When grouting three-dimensional objects or uneven surfaces, it is easiest to spread the grout with a flexible knife or spreader.

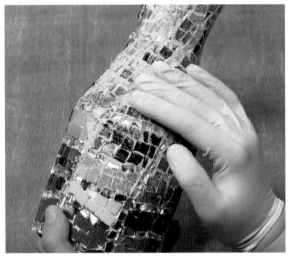

2 Rub the grout deep into the crevices in between the tesserae. Always wear rubber (latex) gloves when you are handling grout directly.

3 To grout large, flat mosaics, you can use powdered tile adhesive. Spoon it on to the surface, then spread it with a soft brush to fill all the crevices between the tesserae.

4 When you have completed the grouting process, spray the tile adhesive with water, using a plastic spray bottle. You may need to repeat the process to achieve a smooth finish.

TEMPLATES

The templates given here can be scaled up or down using a photocopier, to suit the size of your design.

Splashback Squares pp15-17

Valentine Mirror pp22-5

Daisy-covered Table pp18-21

Lemon Tree Floor pp51-5

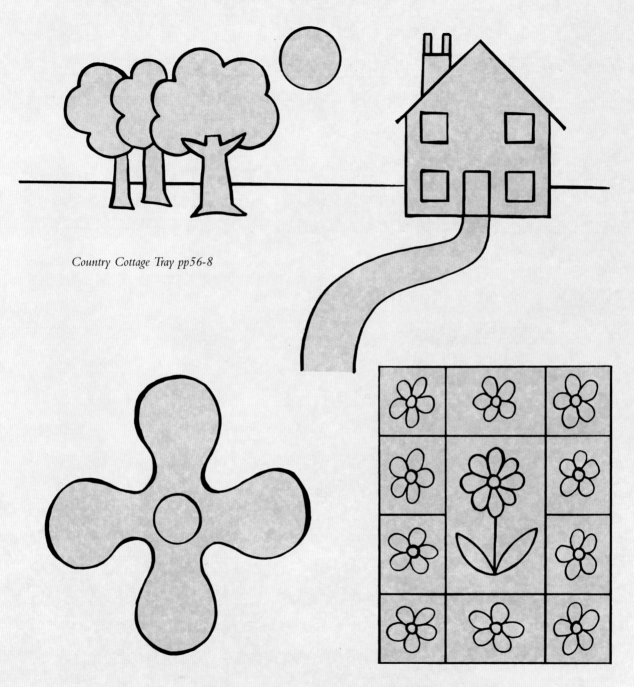

Country Cottage Tray pp56-8

Floral Lamp Base pp59-63

Trinket Box pp67-9

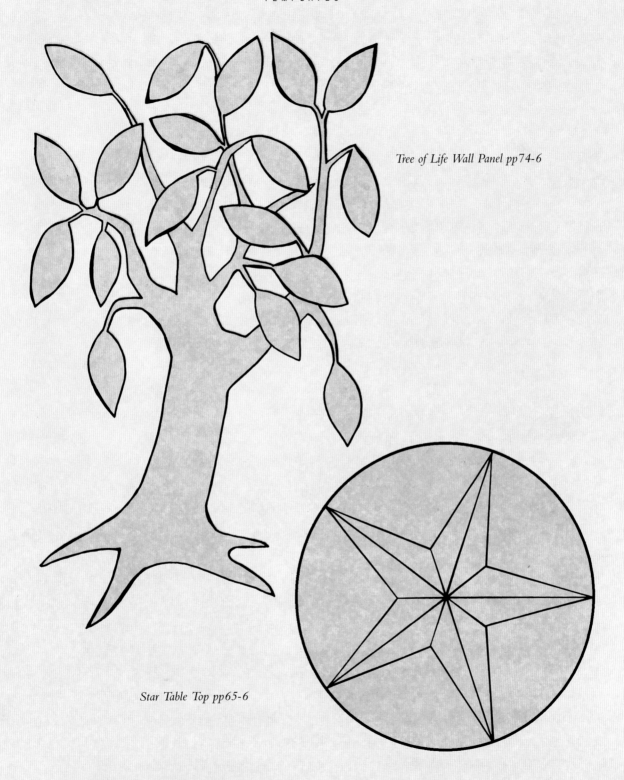

Tree of Life Wall Panel pp74-6

Star Table Top pp65-6

SUPPLIERS

Mosaic requires very few specialist materials or equipment, the majority of which can be found in most do-it-yourself, craft or hardware stores. The suppliers listed here include the better known speciality suppliers, as well as more general suppliers that may be useful, when making the projects illustrated in this book.

UNITED KINGDOM

Mosaic Workshop
1a Princeton Street
London WC1R 4AX
Tel: 0171 404 9249

London Mosaic Weekend
c/o Liz De'Ath
4 Benson Quay
Shadwell
London E1 9TR
Tel: 0171 481 0389

Edgar Udney and Co Ltd
314 Balham High Road
London SW17
Tel: 0181 767 8181

Langley London Ltd
The Tile Centre
161-167 Borough High Street
London SE1 1HU
Tel: 0171 407 4444

Corres Mexican Tiles Ltd
Unit 1A Station Road
Hampton Wick
Kingston
Surrey KT1 4HG
Tel: 0181 943 4142

Worlds End Tiles
Silverthorne Road
Battersea
London SW8 3HE
Tel: 0171 720 8358

The Pot Company
16-20 Raymouth Road
London SE16 2DB
Tel: 0171 394 9711

Tower Ceramics
91 Parkway
Camden Town
London NW1 9PP
Tel: 0171 485 7192

ITALY

Lucio Orsoni
Cannarageio 1045
30121 Venezia
Italy
Tel: 0141 717255

AUSTRALIA

Camden Arts Center Pty Ltd
188-200 Gertrude Street
Fitzroy
Australia 3065

W M Crosbey (Merchandise) Pty
Ltd.
266-274 King Street
Melbourne
Australia 3000

Rodda Pty Ltd
62 Beach Street
Port Melbourne
Victoria
Australia

USA

Alice's Stained Glass
7015 N. 58th Ave.
Glendale, AZ 85301
Tel: (602) 939-7260

Brian's Crafts Unlimited
P.O. Box 731046
Ormond Beach
FL 32173-046
Tel: (904) 672-2726

Ceramica Arnon
134 West 20th St.
New York, NY 10011
Tel: (212) 807-0876

Dick Blick
P.O. Box 1267
Galesburg, IL 61402
Tel: (309) 343-6181

Eastern Art Glass
P. O. Box 341
Wyckoff, NJ 07481
Tel: (201) 847-0001

Hudson Glass Co., Inc
219 N. Division St.
Peekskill, NY 10566
Tel: (914) 737-2124

Ideal Tile of Manhattan, Inc.
405 East 51st St.
New York, NY 10022
Tel: (212) 759-2339

Minnesota/Midwest Clay
8001 Grand Ave. S.
Bloomington, MN 55420
Tel: (612) 884-9101,
(800) 252-9872

S&S
P.O. Box 513
Colchester, CT 06415-0513
Tel: (800) 243-9232

ACKNOWLEDGEMENTS

The Publishers would like to thank the following for the projects photographed in this book:

Helen Baird
Projects: Daisy-covered Table, Decorative Panel, Valentine Mirror, Splashback Squares, Jazzy Plant Pot, Spiral Vase, Trinket Box, Country Cottage Tray, Tree of Life Wall Panel, Floral Lamp Base.

Emma Biggs, Mosaic Workshop
Project: Abstract Mirror.

Sandra Hadfield
Projects: Funky Fruit Bowl, China Rail.

Tessa Hunkin, Mosaic Workshop
Project: Cosmic Clock.

Joanna Nevin
Projects: Stained Glass Candle-holder, Stained Glass Screen.

Norma Vondee
Projects: Lemon Tree Floor, Black-and-White Floor, Star Table Top, Slate Shelf.

The Publishers would like to thank the following companies, who kindly lent items for photography:

Elephant Ltd
94 Tottenham Court Road
London W1P 9HE
Tel: 0171 813 2092

Nice Irma's
46 Goodge Street
London W1P 1FJ
Tel: 0171 580 6921

George Pederson
152 Upper Street
London N1 1RA
Tel: 0171 359 5655

Off the Beaten Track
52 Cross Street
London N1 2BA
Tel: 0171 354 8488

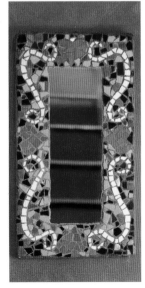

INDEX